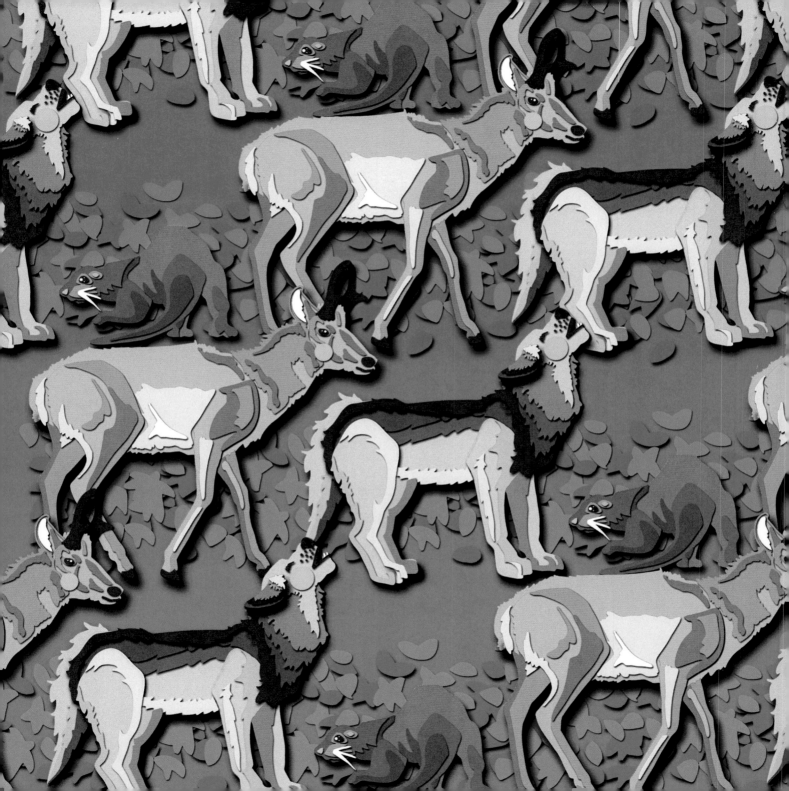

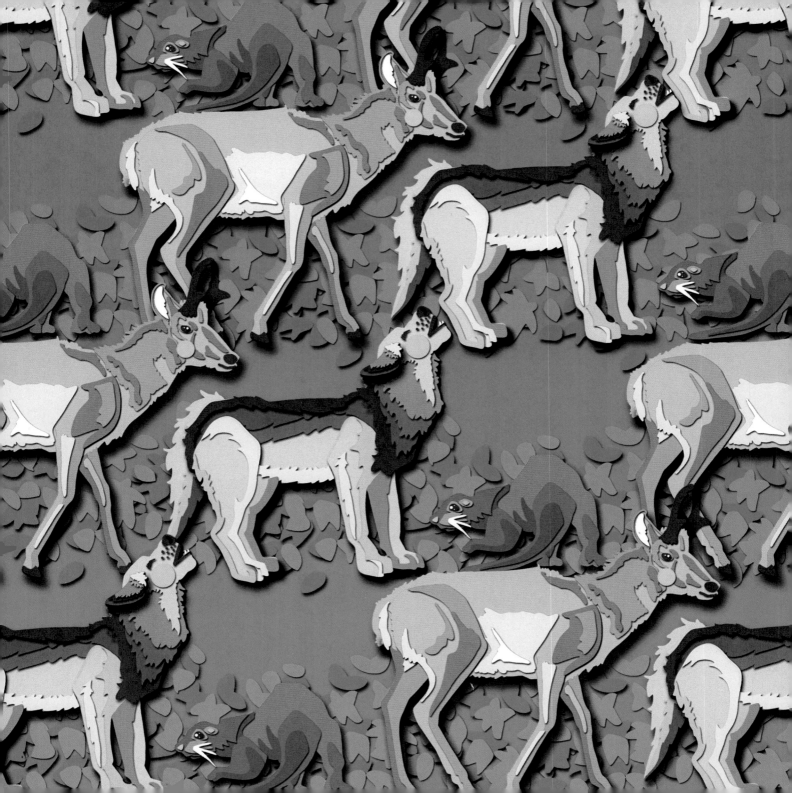

ISBN-13: 978-1732052758

B is for Buffalo
Yellowstone from A to Z

Katy Brown

a is for adventure and
animals of all kinds

b
is for
bison, who are
sometimes called buffalo

is for cubs, courageously climbing quaking aspen

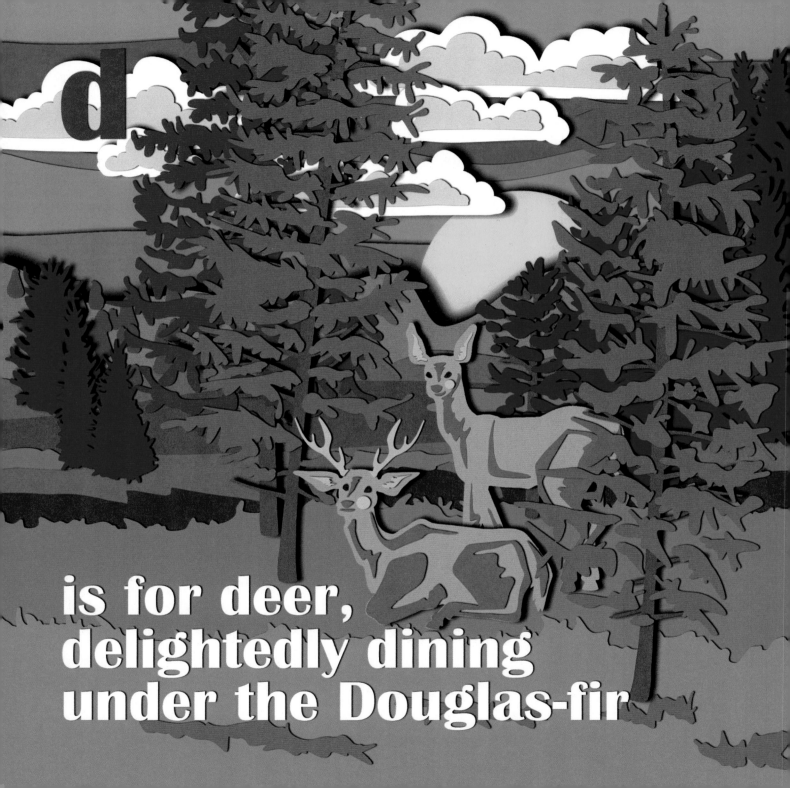

d is for deer, delightedly dining under the Douglas-fir

e is for elk, who enjoy open expanses

is for fox, who frolicks in the freshly frosted forest

g is for geyser that erupts right on schedule

is for inn at Old Faithful, seven stories high

j is for jackrabbit, a hare extraordinaire

k is for kingfisher, crowned
by a colorful crest

L is for lynx,
who lies in wait

m is for mountain goat, who's mighty sure-footed

n is for nuthatches, nestled nicely in a nest

O is for otters, who whirl and swirl and totter

p is for pronghorn, who's practically prancing

q is for quake, so big
it made a lake

is for rattlesnake, who rests on the rocks

S is for sandhill cranes, standing still in a marsh

**is for trout,
who are truly terrific**

u

is for
Undine Falls,
60 feet high

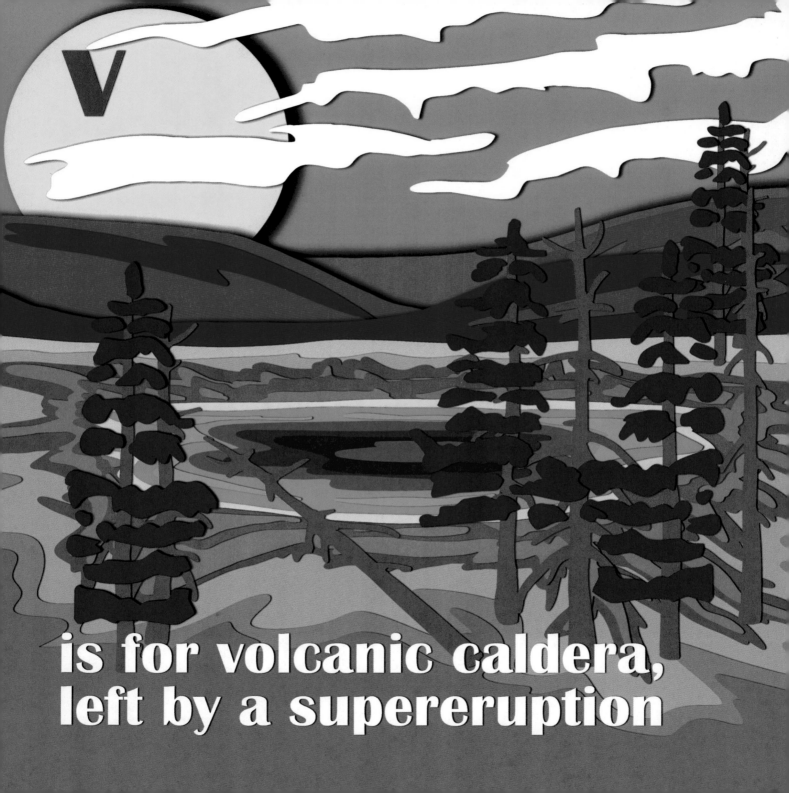

V is for volcanic caldera, left by a supereruption

W is for wolf,
who howls to say howdy

is for extinct, all gone,
like the woolly mammoth

Y is for yellow-bellied marmots, whose young at one are called yearlings

the end

did you know?

- **BUFFALO**, also called bison, are the biggest mammal in North America. They're pretty fast too. They can reach speeds of 30-35 miles an hour!

- The **YELLOWSTONE RED FOX** is small and usually only weighs 10-12 pounds. Boy foxes, or males, are called dogs. Girl foxes, or females, are called vixens.

- **WHITE-TAILED JACKRABBITS** aren't really rabbits at all! They're hares. They're gray-brown in the summer and almost completely white in the winter.

- There are three species of cats found in Yellowstone: **COUGARS, BOBCATS, AND CANADA LYNX.**

- **MOUNTAIN GOATS** have special split hooves perfect for climbing. Both males, called billies, and females, called nannies, have horns and beards!

- **RED-BREASTED NUTHATCHES** have a short, funny song like a horn. It sounds a bit like they're saying, *"yank-yank."*

did you know?

🐾 **YELLOWSTONE RIVER OTTERS** have very sensitive whiskers that help them find food, such as fish and frogs, even underwater. River otters can hold their breath for up to eight minutes.

🐾 **PRAIRIE RATTLESNAKES** are the largest of the six species of reptiles in Yellowstone. Rattlesnakes rattle their tail and hiss as a warning to keep away.

🐾 **WOLVES** like company; they're social animals who live in packs. Packs are usually 6-7 wolves. A howl can be heard from miles away.

🐾 **YELLOW-BELLIED MARMOTS** hibernate for eight months a year. Even though marmots are really ground squirrels, they're sometimes also called "whistle pigs" because they whistle or chirp to sound the alarm and warn others of danger.

🐾 **YELLOWSTONE CUTTHROAT TROUT** are named after the bright red stripes on their jaw or gills. They're a very important *keystone species* in the Park. Many other animals rely on them as a source of food.

Find the animals

Can you find all ten animals in this word search?

```
C T I J X P K Q X Z F N        BISON
B B E V U R Z D X D L E        CRANE
O I C Z F O R A Y E U O        DEER
F S R A P N J G Q E J M        ELK
M O A Z V G B K Z R G H        FOX
G N N U T H A T C H W D        MARMOT
A I E X F O X R W H M M        NUTHATCH
L T V B A R A O G T A T        OTTER
Y V K C B N E U L U R B        PRONGHORN
O S A B E L K T W A M K        TROUT
J K Z U P R V I I S O O
A O T T E R Q G G Z T U
```

Other books by Katy Brown!

Download free coloring pages at www.whatkatydrewnext.com

About the Author

Katy Brown lives in Idaho with her husband, Tyson, and their loyal dog, Lily.

Katy loves reading, sometimes writing (mostly the procrastination of it), and occasionally even drawing. She enjoys sight-seeing in Yellowstone, spending time with friends at Henry's Lake, and lazily floating the Snake River on an inner-tube.

This is her second picture book.

Lily, also called Pig or Piggy, is a Vizsla. She loves running, digging holes, and eating spoils that fall on the kitchen floor. Lily dog especially loves carrots, walks, and burrowing into the blankets at bedtime.

Visit www.whatkatydrewnext.com to see all upcoming book releases.

Follow @whatkatydrewnext on Instagram & Facebook to see what Katy, Tyson, and Lily are doing next.

Enjoy even more!

Color along in this educational coloring book! *Wildlife of the West* by Katy Brown features 33+ coloring pages showcasing animals and pastimes of the Intermountain West. Add a personal touch to the outdoors with this fact-filled activity book. Older children are sure to love the companion color-by-number book, *Nature by Number*.

Download free coloring pages at www.whatkatydrewnext.com

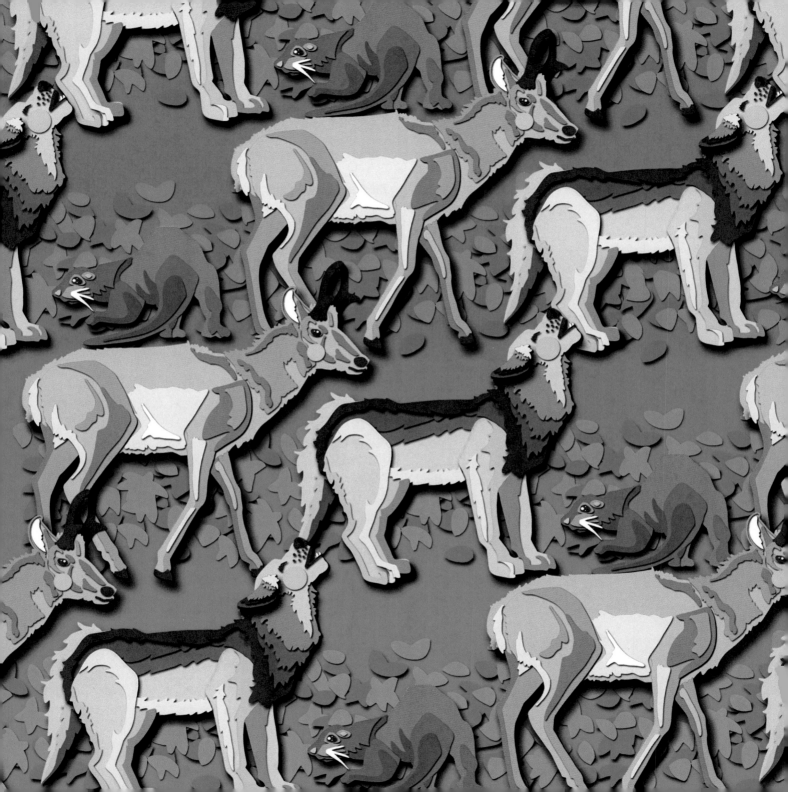

Made in the USA
Las Vegas, NV
06 May 2022

48429616R00026